WORKING CLASS REPRESENT

BY CRISTIN O'KEEFE APTOWICZ

A Write Bloody Book
Long Beach, CA USA

Working Class Represent
a collection of poetry

ɔʒ

by Cristin O'Keefe Aptowicz

Write Bloody Publishing
America's Independent Press

Long Beach, CA

writebloody.com

Aptowicz, Cristin O'Keefe.
1st edition.
ISBN: 978-1-935904-72-4

Interior Layout by Lea C. Deschenes
Cover Designed by Joshua Grieve
Proofread by Sarah Kay
Edited by Derrick Brown and Sarah Kay
Author Photo by Alex Brook Lynn
Type set in Helvetica by Linotype and Bergamo (www.theleagueofmoveabletype.com)

Special thanks to Lightning Bolt Donor, Weston Renoud

Printed in Tennessee, USA

Write Bloody Publishing
Long Beach, CA
Support Independent Presses
writebloody.com

To contact the author, send an email to writebloody@gmail.com

WORKING CLASS REPRESENT

THE HAPPY FUN OF LOVE

$356 in my bank account, yo!
And my parents work for the government!

I'm living La Vida Frozen Pierogi
at the intersection of Un-hire-able-ness
and Writer's Block!

Wanna come over?

This poem is supposed to be funny.

If you are not laughing,
I'll list that as yet another failure.

CO-WORKERS

I can never make it in on time.
The trains are always screwed up in the mornings,
and I didn't even have time to get my coffee.
Ugh, I don't know how other people do it,
those early people with their coffees.

And I just need a little personal time
right at the top, just need to straighten out
a few things: make that doctor's appointment,
cancel my landline, call back my mom
because I got her message late last night
and I just couldn't call her back. Honestly,
I feel so much better and ready to work
once I get that stuff out of the way.

And why can't people make sense in their emails?
Why can't they just read what I send them and
then write back what I ask for? That's all.
It's not that hard. Why is everyone an idiot?

And God, I hope I don't get caught again
printing out fliers for my band here. I mean,
the hours I work, the time I give, I certainly
earned the—what?—three cents these copies
cost the company? But God, I hate getting caught.
Like I need that lecture. Again. *I know.*

And does anyone know if we are getting off
for President's Day? I can't remember if we did
last year. But it would be nice to know, either way;
we always find out these things too late,
and I never have a chance to get out of the city.

And they say that you should be dressing
for the job you want, not the job that you have.
Which is why I dress the way I do: I barely want
this job, and I certainly don't want whatever job
is above this job. Whatever that even means.

And this isn't what I want to do forever, you know,
but I like it here. As jobs go, it's not so bad.

ODE TO MY MORNING CUP OF COFFEE

I buy you every morning at the same place.
They know me there, and have the cup
ready before I even approach the counter.

Some days the subway acts up, and I run
so late that I don't have time to pick you up.
We categorize those days as being "bad."

Life without you, coffee, wouldn't be a life at all.
It would be a terrible fog, a slow-motion movie
about the wind, the world's driest muffin

choked down with a paper cup of warm water.
It would be me actually kicking a trashcan
after yelling at a fax machine when the truth is,

I'm the one who keeps dialing the wrong number.
I need you, coffee, and I don't think that part
of our relationship is unhealthy. It's good to need

things in your life and I need you, morning cup
of coffee, I need you *so much*. You don't even know.
Look at me! Look at my eyes! Do you see how serious

I am? Coffee, I would take a bullet for you. I would
wear your burns like a badge of honor. I would punch
a tea bag in the face, and not shed a single tear.

MONDAY MORNING

Everyone pretends they hate Mondays:
Got a case of the Mondays, they say.

But as work mornings go, I believe
Monday mornings are the best.

This is contrary, I know,
to what most office workers think.

But Monday mornings,
you tend to be better rested,

and you have a fresh start
when it comes to your wardrobe,

which is helpful when you like
to wear the same things all the time,

like me. Nothing tastes as good
as Monday morning coffee.

Everyone has something to talk about
from their weekend: the weather,

the movies, the meals, the trips,
the hangovers, the arguments, the excess

or lack of sleep, those sweet, small things
we identify as our lives outside of work.

COMPUTER GUY

You work part-time, so we tend not
to include you in our office Secret Santa.
You are good humored about it, and bring
us all holiday peanut brittle by the bucketful.

We do celebrate your birthday,
but let's be honest: we are an office
of women, so that probably has more
to do with the free cake than with you.

You work in an office with no windows,
and your door opens to an empty space.
We frequently are unaware if you are
even there, buzzing your phone tentatively,

genuinely surprised when you answer.
You once called out of work for three days
because your wife was giving birth
to your second child. We all had to confess

that we didn't know you had a wife,
nor that she was pregnant, let alone
with a second child. I don't even think
we signed an office card for you.

Despite all of it, the simple fact is
that you, part-time computer guy,
get the most hugs per capita
of anyone in the office.

You remind us to update our AntiVirus,
you replace our cracked monitors,
our coffee-soaked keyboards, and shine
brightest at our meltdown moments:

our eyes fuzzy with tears, our hands shaking
over a file stuck, or deleted, or God knows what.
You send us to get coffee for ourselves
and when we return, everything is fine,

perfect, like new, or rather like old.
And you shrug, offering simple tech advice
which we will immediately forget,
squeezing you tightly, relieved.

We promise ourselves to remember your birthday.
Next time, we promise to get you a great gift.

RULES OF SLACK

Times when it is okay not to work
while you are at work include

times you're not feeling well
if you are sick, or overtired

from something not related to partying,
or playing a medium-sized gig with your band,

or hosting your poetry slam series.
If your boyfriend breaks your heart,

you can get away with doing
absolutely nothing at all, but if you do try

to bury yourself in work, you'll be rewarded
with a small bag of your favorite candy.

It's generally acceptable not to work
when the boss is on vacation, but you

shouldn't be open about it. On a practical level,
it's also okay to ease off of work when

you have a timely or boring personal chore:
a GYN appointment to schedule, plane tickets home

to price and buy, canceling a gym membership.
Fun chores, such as buying Christmas gifts

for friends, or googling old boyfriends,
are not acceptable reasons to slack.

But for me, I have my own standards
for when it's okay to stray from my

usually tenacious office work ethic.
It includes the first 45 minutes after you arrive

before the coffee hits, the last 45 minutes
before you leave when the coffee's run out,

and anytime, like now, when a boring poem
bites you in the hand, and refuses to shake off.

I'M TOO SEXY FOR THIS OFFICE

When you pay your way through college,
much of your time is spent working, and
much of the money you make is already
accounted for before it hits your bank account.

To say that I didn't care about fashion
would be an understatement. In college,
I had one pair of shoes: Payless boots.
I had two pairs of Dickies pants in black,

two pairs of pajama bottoms that could
sort of pass as real pants in the summer,
and two pairs of thrift store brown slacks
which my friends called "the old man pants."

My shirts were all bought at either TJ Maxx
or Walmart, or were given to me by my mother
at Christmas. I think most students make
the choice to either look their age, or to look

professional. They just suck it up and do it.
So what if they're too hip for their cubicle?
Who cares if their classmates think they look
like sell-outs, like middlemen, like office drones?

But me, I struck down the middle. I looked
awkward in both worlds. And this is true:
one day, I was approached by a reality TV
fashion makeover show and they asked me

to describe my style. I told them: *Bad Employee*.
They smiled and asked, *Do you mean 'partying
all night?' bad? Or 'I'm too sexy for this office' bad?
Or 'I don't give a fuck what the boss says' bad?*

and I thought, what jobs do these people have?
Something tells me they've never bought their shirts
by the pound, or purchased pants solely based
on how well they will camouflage coffee stains.

ANSWERING THE PHONES

I have answered the phones
at every job I've ever had.

I owe it to the fact
that I have a sunny disposition,

a natural love of enunciation,
and an unabashed eagerness

at the sound of a ringing bell.

TEAM SPIRIT

I am the girl who starts the birthday song
at the office birthday parties.

I bring in the homemade holiday cookies
in the shape of dachshunds

because everyone knows I love dachshunds,
as my cubicle clearly shows.

I make your high fives feel less awkward.
I applaud at the end of every meeting.

I will tell you, new co-worker,
not to worry, that it took me a long time

to figure out the copy machine too, and about how
I loudly fell out of my chair on my first day.

I am the one who makes funny announcements
on the office-wide PA system.

I am the team player, I am your cheerleader,
I am the one who, when things get stressful,

will bite my lower lip, point at you with both fingers,
and say, *You know what? That's why I love this job.*

DAY JOB

I.
It's Monday, and I began writing this poem
in my head on the way to work, pressed
into the subway so tightly, all I could do
was stare at my own reflection in the glass,
the tunnel rocketing by, the woman next
to me holding her coffee in her hands
like prayer.

II.
I like to tell people I need this: my job
like a ruler rapping against my knuckles
every morning, Monday through Friday.
It keeps me centered, I say, focused.
I can create for the sake of creating,
I don't need to equate my art with money.
Makes me feel vital, like a working artist.
Make me feel like I'm working.

III.
My friend tells me he thinks I'm cowardly
for clinging to my cubicle, my free printing,
my air-conditioning, my health insurance,
my payroll, my tax forms, my dress codes,
my forty-five minute commutes, my Secret
Santas, my birthday cakes, my spreadsheets,
my official title to be included on every piece
of correspondence. I love it, I tell him.
I can't imagine life without it.

IV.
I think I used to be a funnier poet.

V.
When I was six, I had a severe allergic reaction
to the trees in Yellowstone Park. My eyelids
swelled up so much that I couldn't see. Later,
my mom tried to cook fish over a campfire
and failed. I bit into the burnt trout and asked:
*Are you trying to feed me tree bark? Because
I might be blind, but I can still tell the difference.*
My mom said, if I was still able to joke around,
then my condition must not be that serious,
and I remember thinking, *For God's sake,
you are blind! Do not make any more jokes!*

VI.
I don't know how this story
relates to the rest of this poem,
except that, of course I do.

DEAR WHOEVER IS SENDING PICTURES TO MY PHONE

My phone is not fancy enough to receive photos.
You are probably sending me photos of something
funny and sweet or something that reminds you of me,
but in reality, all you are really sending me is a reminder
that I am too poor to afford a fancy phone. My phone
won't even tell me who is sending these photos.
It only tells me a photo has been sent, and guess what!
I'm too poor to see it, so *ha-ha*. In the *New Yorker* cartoon
of this poem, I would be portrayed by an old labrador.
I would be so out of it that I would be complaining
to a lumpy ottoman, thinking it was another dog.

SEX APPEAL

Today, someone in my office said,
Well, don't you look nice today!
I replied, *Thanks, but it wasn't intentional,*
which in retrospect sounded rude.

But really, it was the truth.
Last night, I realized that my goal
is to be attractive enough to have it
not be an issue. No more, no less.

When someone asks someone I know,
Is Cristin good looking?
I want them to think about it, like
they never really considered it before.

Then I want them to respond, *Well,*
I wouldn't kick her out of a car.
That's what I want: to be just
attractive enough to stay in the car.

HEART SWEATER

The day they sold sweaters for $5 on a table
on Fifth Avenue was also the day all the ladies
in the office decided to pool money together
and buy me, the intern, some new things to wear.

The worst looking sweater was given to me
by the sweetest member of the staff, Ginny,
who'd make an extra pan of cornbread just
for me when she cooked for her church.

The sweater was bright purple, with pink and
red hearts stitched across the chest. It wasn't
until I got home that I saw that she had tucked
a brand new tube of toothpaste in the sleeve.

What do these people think of me? I wondered,
spilling the garbage bag of sweaters on my floor.
I stared at the pile, feeling a bit mixed up: worried
they thought I was worse off than I thought I was,

but so grateful at the new things I had to wear,
at the huge tube of toothpaste: plump and new,
just waiting to be squeezed.

CLOSE OUT SALE

Turns out things aren't going that well.
Turns out you wake up and you're thirty,
and the clothes you are wearing aren't ironic
anymore. They are the clothes you wear.

One day you wake up, and look in your closet
and realize it is every terrible thing your mother
ever said to you, all cut from 100% poly-blend.

These are the days your shoes dissolve in the rain,
the days your boss asks if that's a hole in your pants,
and you don't even have to look down to confirm.

These are the days you pin a poem to the page
just to see it stare back at you, gasping for air.

WRITE A POEM ABOUT MONSTERS

is the note I found in my email inbox this morning,
mailed from none other than myself. I do this now
when a poem keeps me up, I email myself a note
so I can sleep, wake, and go to work with a poem
already waiting for me at the other end.

Sometimes it's successful, but other times
the notes just don't make sense the next morning.
Poem about Neck Face probably didn't burst
into poetic flame within me quite the same way
my nighttime self had probably hoped it would.

Twin Sestinas for Twins was another seemingly
good idea that couldn't shake itself up, a wet colt
I didn't have the interest to lick to its feet.
This note, *Write a Poem about Monsters*, is
another one I'm not sure I'll ever write right.

See, when I was a kid, I tried to will ghosts
to swarm my house, rise torso-less from ponds,
pop from inside bathroom mirrors. Each hike,
a chance to see Big Foot; every beach,
a possible landing place for Nessie.

I once spent an entire summer afternoon
trying to move a pen using only my mind.
These are the things you do when you are
young, bored, and have access to Time-Life's
Mysteries of the Unknown book series—

a book series I had to beg my mother for,
a book series I considered so precious, I read them
only when wearing gloves. And my midnight note,
Write a Poem about Monsters, was written hoping
that when morning broke across my desk, and

coffee shook the rumpled bed of my brain, I'd find
something profound in this obsession. But instead,
I just find more nothing, another ghost of a poem
to throw in the grave with Neck Face, another pen
I swore I could move with only my brain,

but couldn't.

DAY JOB II

It's hard to take a vow
of silence when your day job
is answering phones.

Sometimes I want to write
autobiographical essays about
my obsessive collecting
of dachshund figurines. Other times,
I'd rather get the sleep.

I've spent two hours looking up
the home and office addresses of writers
I admire, and zero hours writing them.

Sometimes the fire of a poem
wisps out the moment I take out the pen.

Sometimes I think I just need to get away,
break schedule, shake things up,
but other times I remember:

that's exactly what people say
when they are trying to avoid work.

SPRING AND BROADWAY

One of the perils of working in SoHo is
all the models who clump down the street
in impossible shoes, pulling their black
binders to their chest, chatting in Italian
or French or Russian on tiny cell phones.
Every woman who passes just stares
at their thighs—which never ever touch—
zipped into skinny jeans or latex leggings.

Fashion Week is like an M.C. Escher
drawing, with an endless line of models
cat-walking down the sidewalk, identical
black binders, Avant-garde jackets, and
those thin, thin thighs. Those weeks, I feel
like a troll, short and disheveled, hurrying
down the street in my urchin's clothes.

On the subway ride back to Queens, I grow
several inches, lose several pounds, regain
the effortless hip of my dollar store clothes,
my bargain bin shoes. Or not. Sometimes,
I come home the troll too and that's okay.
Or, you know, not.

DAY JOB III

I am tired of writing about my shoes.

I am tired of wearing my shoes,
but writing about them has proven
even more tiresome, even to me—
and they are my shoes.

The world gets it: cheap shoes means
you don't got money. The world gets it:
I don't got money. What poet does?

Answer: quite a few, actually.
I've gone to their readings and seen their shoes.
they don't look like mine, I can tell you that.

My college professor told me that work is good:
good for the soul and good for writing too.
When you are forced to make room
for writing in a day already crammed with subways,
and bosses, and cranky customers,

your writing time means more to you,
and so you get more writing done—better writing
too, hopefully. But it is hard to feel empowered
stuffed into an overheated subway car
forty-five minutes every A.M. and another forty-five
every P.M, wearing the same winter coat you've worn
for the last eight winters.

You just feel poor. You feel poor still.
You begin to feel you will be poor forever.

And this is where my friend Taylor would tell me
the poem needs a dénouement, a solid reversal,
a part where the poet (me) realizes her own value
and the value of her work; she stops bemoaning
her old shoes and unraveling coat (which has held up!
Even after eight winters!) and instead celebrates
how full and wonderful her life is, in so many ways.

But instead of all that, how about I tell you this:
my friend Taylor is rich—born that way—and sometimes
he gives me his good advice while driving his hybrid car
to his country house, while I sit at my small beige cubicle,
wearing my same old shoes, staring at the clock
like it was a wailing baby, one that I stopped
wanting to comfort hours ago.

PERSONAL FINANCES

This morning my breakfast cost fifty cents,
and that fact has made me feel proud all day.

I now have more in savings than I make in a year
at my job, but I'm afraid to leave my job.

Once that savings is gone, it is gone,
and it was so hard to save.

I really love doing research-heavy writing projects,
but do I love it more than having health insurance?

Some days, I realize that I need to stop
buying my work clothes at dollar stores.

Other days, I think of all the money I save
by buying my work clothes at dollar stores

and how that money will come in handy
when I am fired for wearing cheap, inappropriate

clothing at my office job. Or, you know,
when I just fucking quit already.

THE LONG GREEN UMBRELLA

On rainy days, I hold it across my legs when I ride
the subway, like the lap-bar for a very boring rollercoaster.
When I exit, the umbrella is a cane, and I climb the stairs
like a grand doyenne. On the street, it becomes a baton,

a pointing stick, an unstable pole to vault me over puddles.
Sometimes it snags in a hidden grate, twangs out of my hand
like a sudden, insistent tree. In the elevator, the umbrella drips
like a fresh cut orchid, weeps like a lonesome woman.

At the office, I refuse to put it with the rest of the umbrellas
in the trashcan by the door. Too awkward and tall, all day
it would be knocked to the ground, snagged on coats, cursed.
So I keep it by my desk, flat against the side of my cubicle.

As the day goes on, it dries out next to me, losing its shine.
It almost blends in. I try to remember where I got it, finally
recalling the lost and found box at the bar. How it was still
early, but already it rattled with abandonment.

Take any one you want, the bartender said. *People always
leave them behind, never come back.* All identical: compact,
disposable, easy to break. *Or*, he said, *you can take that one.*
There it was: long and bright and weird, so close to the garbage

I actually gasped. I remember I walked right up to it.
I remember I grabbed it. I remember I claimed it as mine.

9/11

Lucky Kim, my roommate, is sleeping
next to me after 13 hours
of solid television coverage.

She is the only person I have seen,
waking me up in the morning, asking:
What are your plans for today,
because two planes just crashed
into the World Trade Center.

Lucky Kim, who works
at the World Financial Center,
stayed home today and got the news
between her morning run and cracking
open her books for study.

Together, we watch the news
and she points out her building
attached to the towers
by gory amputated bridges,
windows shattered, metal buckled.

For hours,
we call her friends, coworkers:

busy signals, no answers.

I run out for juice and donuts
and after that, we eat, drink,
and lean in to each other,
in front of the TV.

We only have one channel now,
all the rest went down with the towers.
And the computers and telephones join the TV
in a parade of whirling ineffectiveness:
What's happening? What's happening?

Heads hungry for information,
we dumbly watch the plane bank
again and again into deadly blossom,
listen to the survivors, watch
the dust people run from the rumble,
our hands on the phone, waiting,
waiting.

We watch.
All of lower Manhattan,
all of New York City,
consumed in this cloud:
dirt, paper, plaster, people.

LAST MEAL

I suppose it comes as no surprise that when the nation
faces a crisis, and one's own existence is no longer
a guarantee, that we, the pasty-faced, out-of-shape,
CNN-addicted anxiety junkies would talk about food.

My friends and I, too sad to talk about the bitter hard
of our hearts and the event which cut our calloused country
to the quick, decide instead to talk about our last meals—
what they would be, if we could choose them. For me,

after much debate, I settle on the following:
grilled cheese, half Fontina and half Cheddar,
on thick-cut, crusty, buttered sour dough bread,
with round, ruby red slices of fresh Jersey tomatoes;

mashed potatoes, skin-on, beat with cream and butter,
left lumpy, with salt and pepper to taste; creamed spinach,
thick, garlicky, dotted with small opaque onion squares
and served hot; and lastly, sweet potato casserole,

made with honeyed sweet potatoes, cinnamon, nutmeg,
marshmallows, butter, and a brown sugar crumble crust.
Unlimited supplies of all of the above, to be drunk
with coffee from my favorite diner in Philadelphia.

With all the culinary options provided by restaurants and mothers
and grandmothers and crafty boyfriends and Martha Stewart
glossy magazine spreads like pornography for the glutton,
I was surprised at how simple my last meal would be.

So I decided to cut to the chase and make the full meal
on the first cold, rainy night of autumn, so I would never
regret not eating that meal, so carefully laid out to be my last.
However, on my way to the grocery store, head filled

with images of the dinner to come, I was nearly struck dead,
walking blindly into rain-slick traffic. It was then I realized:
eating your last meal because it's rainy and cold,
and you are sad and scared, is just kind of asking for it.

ALL I'D LEAVE BEHIND

My mother has always been very laissez-faire about death:
When it's your time, it's your time. Nothing you can do about it.
Sharing this philosophy has helped me through many mornings
in this city when everything seems too quiet. Like the morning

after the London bombings when the subways rattled empty
in what should have been the morning rush. My car held me
and five people, all of whom were reading bibles. I thought,
If it's your time, it's your time… and counted down my stops.

Living in New York City, it's too easy to imagine you'll die
in an act of violence just going to work. It's scary and a bit
egotistical, as if the sight of me in business casual is enough
to make someone press their small button. But you never know.

And so sometimes, I think about what would be left behind,
if I were to evaporate into all that angry, burning air: the letters
left unstamped, the half-finished poems, my wandering outlines.
The morning after the bombings, I realized that my bag held

three books, all on the lives of serial killers. Grim research
for a writing project, sure, but I admit I nearly laughed out loud
thinking about rescuers who would find me, how they'd look
in my bag and think, *Whoa, maybe this one was for the best…*

Gallows humor, I suppose, for a dark time, but it's proof
of what I know is true— this: My city still glitters despite it all.
All that hard-edged fearlessness, those worn bibles on laps,
the cups of coffee sipped from shaking hands. We still shine.

And if it's my time, it's my time. Nothing I can do, but do
what I'm doing now, write what I'm writing now, so if that
dark day comes, the people at my office might smile
when they clean out my desk—its messy collection

of grant applications and dizzy comics—and maybe pause
to wonder at the post-it note still stuck in my drawer, a line
copied from a book of ancient Chinese poetry which reads:

Today, at last, a letter came,
and I've lit my lamp a hundred times
to read its words of love.

IN THE MOVIE OF MY LIFE
I SOMETIMES IMAGINE

In the opening credits, I am riding the subway.
It's a montage of all of my morning commutes.
My clothing and the books I'm reading change,
but everything else stays pretty much the same.

My character is weary: disheveled but determined.
The montage itself is supposed to reflect life's
monotony, but there's pockets of humor too:
the mornings I'm so tired I don't realize I am

holding my book upside down; the times
I've accidentally worn my sweater inside out
and backwards, the small pale tag hanging
like a flag of surrender at my throat; how

I like to make eye contact with dogs in bags,
their wet noses pressed against the mesh. Still,
it's clear the movie is not a thin comedy. There
is a real person here. I'm a real person here.

I tend to fantasize about this movie the most
while I'm on the subway—pretend I am being
filmed, angle my face to just left of where
I imagine the camera should be. I pause

to let viewers see me, really see me. My brain's
director tells me my motivation. I am to think:
ambitious. Sometimes, *deserving*. I tend to think:
struggling. Sometimes, *useless*. But I push

through it. And then, at the perfect moment,
I swing my head right, look past the camera
into what I assume is my triumphant future.
I imagine this is where the film cuts to black,

where the opening credits end and the real meat
of the movie begins. Only, I have no idea what
is supposed to happen next. I haven't gotten
that far. So instead, I go back to the opening:

me in the subway again. Me in the subway still.
Sometimes I try to figure out what music should
play over the opening credits. Is it happy? Is it sad?
Will it make any difference at all?

BRUSHES WITH FAME

Some guy who worked at my boyfriend's old bookstore
(the chain store, not the independent) got nominated
for an Oscar for acting. Another guy who worked
at my boyfriend's old bookstore (the independent one,
not the chain store) has a big fan in Brooklyn: we kept
seeing stickers of his band everywhere. An old friend's
ex-girlfriend (the high schooler, not the former model)
went to school with the lady rapper who did the song
about her milkshake, and the non-specified ways
it brought all the boys to the yard. For six months
I worked as an assistant for a famous painter.
I'd sweep her studio, clean the litter box, organize
her paint tubes by color. It was my job to take out
the trash, and sometimes I would marvel at the sketches
she threw in the trash, wondering if I'd get in trouble
if I took them, wondering what I'd even do with them,
if it was morally right to hang an artist's garbage as art.
I didn't take anything, but wanted to: I like first drafts.
I like how they seem so infused with potential,
how they just want to be given a chance.

THANK YOU FOR YOUR INTEREST IN OUR FELLOWSHIP

Oh, failure. We meet again here
on the kitchen floor. It's where
I sprawl, generic rejection letter
sitting on my chest like a dead pigeon.

The lightbulb gets screwy then clear,
screwy then clear, screwy then clear,
as my eyes leak their stupid parade,
all that wet, misplaced hope.

Ain't I the hypocrite? Ain't I
always the one pushing pushing
pushing, always telling people
to see the best parts of themselves,

to put it on paper, and send it out,
see what fate has to say about it?
So who else did I expect to see
in the polished brass of rejection,

but my worst self, my weakest,
my most self-pitying, holding up
rejection letters as if they were
road maps that only told me exits,

and never the on ramps, never
how to get where I want to go.

ODE TO THE PEOPLE WHO HAVE REJECTED MY WORK

I know that it's not easy to be you. The piles
of work you must read: the poems, the essays,
the heartfelt, if utterly overblown cover letters.

The electric potential must turn pretty quickly
to heavy dread. I've been known to kiss
an envelope before mailing it. I sometimes

picture them in the mailbox: eager candles,
just waiting to glow. And yes, your teachers
are right: rejection is not the end of the world,

though some nights it can feel like it. I admit
to eating sorry bowls of creamed spinach,
sulking on my kitchen floor, too sad to move:

Oh, the rejection! Oh, my mashed dreams!
But I don't blame you, dear editor. I'm sure
it's no fun to be the one judging, especially

when your efforts must feel so unappreciated.
No one publishes your carefully crafted refusals,
except jerks who mock them in their dumb blogs;

no one compliments your witty yet specific
submission guidelines, in fact, it seems like
no one even reads them; and you must get

so tired, so desperately tired. I mean, you
have to be absolutely bone weary, perhaps
even in a coma, a coma caused by idiocy,

to reject the bedazzled genius in honeyed
poetry as straightforwardly genuine as mine.
I'm kidding, of course. Not about my genius,

but about the blame. I totally blame you
for rejecting me. Absolutely. 100%.
P.S. these stains you see are real tears.

NOTES ON REJECTION(S)[1]

Almost there, but no!
Not Quite!
Not These!
So close—top 10%!!
Really tempting, but we're going to have to pass!
Focus more on language, less on story!
Horrible, like a textbook—meaning it sounds like it's been copied
     from a textbook!
Addresses the theme, but SO WHAT?
No!
Not good!
So Funny! I actually laughed out loud at some lines! But no!
We apologize for this rejection arriving so close to the holidays, but...
Sorry!
I'm sorry!
Sorry!
We're Sorry!
Sorry!
Try again!
Keep submitting!
We are sure you'll find a home for at least one of these...
The theme of our next issue is "Failure,"
and it seems like you might have a lot of poems about that!

---

1 This is a found poem composed from actual notes on or in actual rejection letters
I've received over the years.

TO THE GUY WHO SAID FUNNY POETRY AIN'T POETRY

So you don't think funny poetry is poetry, huh?
Is that it? You don't think funny poetry is poetry.

Wow. That's a real cause to step against.
You're really saving lives with that one.
Emaciated premature babies from inside tiny iron lungs
raise their frail arms to you. Dying nuns open cracked lips
to offer benedictions in your name. And somewhere
in heaven, your grandmother is smiling with pride, saying,
Thank you, Jesus, that my baby is the one to finally tell
the world that funny poetry isn't poetry!

What kind of simple-minded, uncultured prick
do you have to be to claim you know so much about poetry
that you alone can dictate what is and isn't poetry, and yet
be so uneducated as to not recognize the long literary history
of humorous poetry, you fucking dick suck condom head mouth?

Remember Shakespeare, that old asshole? Remember him, *genius*?
Remember how he wrote that:
if snow be white, / why then his lover's breasts are dun?
Or that:
if hairs be wires, / black wires grow on her head?
or what about:
And in some perfumes is there more delight
Than in the breath that from my mistress reeks.

You know what that is? That is Shakespeare being purposefully
insensitive and obtuse in order to gain the audience reaction
that he wanted. And what was that reaction?

Laughter, motherfucker, laughter!

Or what about Langston Hughes, who wrote:
I swear to the Lord, / I still can't see,
Why Democracy means, / Everybody but me.

Or Dorothy Parker who mused that:
If you want to know what God thinks of money,
just look at the people he gave it to.

Or T.S. Elliot who wrote:
Some editors are failed writers,
but so are most writers.

And praise on high, Ogden Nash!

Candy is dandy,
but liquor is quicker.

The problem with kittens
is that they turn into cats.

Or my personal favorite:
I think that I shall never see
a billboard lovely as a tree.
Perhaps, unless the billboards fall,
I'll never see a tree at all.

These are poets. These are writers. And you say
my stage is a comedy club, and you say that funny poets
aren't poets, and you say my examples are unfair,
spotlighting poets who happen to write funny things,
not comedians fronting that they can write poetry.

But if you are going to use their words against them,
I'll use your words against you. Because a person
who denies another person that they can write poetry
is an *asshole*. And a person who tries to humilate
a person just trying to express themselves is a *bully*.
And a person who tries to silence poetry simply
because it makes people laugh is a fucking *tyrant*.

Because seriously, how hard is it to make someone sad?
Your mother is ugly. Is that a poem?

But to make someone laugh is a gift. To take a bad day
and crack it over some sharp verse, pull from that shell
a smile, a giggle, a guffaw? That, my friend, is a talent
whose respect should never be denied.

So if you need to take someone on, take me on,
Little Man Serious, because I can handle you.

I'll make you laugh so hard, your ego will burst.
I'll school you in ha-ha so serious, your funny bone
will dissolve into your urine.

So you listen to me: Don't you dare tell poets
what they can and cannot write, let alone in my house,
against my friends. Because not only will I take you on,
but guess what? I have an army. A very funny army.

A very funny army that does not just consist of funny poets,
because my borders are endless: funny poets and serious poets,
political poets and hip-hop poets, experimental poets
and old schoolers. I embrace the inherent poetry
of every motherfucker I see, whether they call themselves
poets or not. So let it be known once and for all:

Richard Pryor is a poet! And Lenny Bruce is a poet!
And Charles Schultz, creator of Peanuts, is a haiku genius!

And every person in this room is a poet!
And every person reading this book is a poet!
And every person who has the breath and the heart
and guts to say that they are a poet, are all poets
because who am I to say that they aren't?

And if you call yourself a poet, and espouse hateful shit
like *funny poetry ain't poetry* one more time,
I'm going to flip the script and get serious on your ass.

And you don't want my grim prose
all knocking up on your face, so why don't you just
step back and actually listen for a moment:

open your mind,
open your heart,
open your mouth,

and just laugh.

MOVIES I WANT TO SEE MADE

1.) *Beavie McBeaver*
This movie features a beaver as a protagonist, like a beaver who gets in to college and people think he is a genius because he speaks and takes notes, you know, because he's a beaver and they can't do that shit! Hot girls want to sleep with him, and hot guys get bad self-esteem around him, and it ends with him wearing an ascot and a smoking jacket. He has become the president of the college. He looks in the camera and says—and mind you he's never spoken for this whole film, *not a sound!*—he looks into the camera and says: *Who'd a fucking thought it: I'm a fucking beaver.* And also, it's a documentary.

2.)This one's got a great title: *Mother Effin' Wiener Dogs!*
It's a film about wiener dogs. Cool ass wiener dogs. Cool ass wiener dogs that fuck mothers.

3.) *Everybody's Gay*
This gay fantasia would star all the guys who I liked and who didn't like me back. Now they are all gay and fucking each other in front of me indefinitely. Forever. And it's filmed in real time.

4.) *Chicky Dick's Lucky Duck and the Case of the Nefarious Kitten*
Pretty Self-Explanatory.

5.) Here are some other great titles:

Late Night Cable Access Shows: The Musical

7th Grade: The Musical

Me Being Able to Pay the Bills: The Musical

NPR: The Porn

Keeping It Real: The Musical

Keep It Wrong: The Musical

When Am I Going to Blow Up?: The Musical

*Seriously, It's Been Two Years Since I Graduated College
and Look at Me, I Look Like a Hobo: The Musical*

I'll Do Anything Not to Be Poor: The Porn

Please God Help Me Out: The Musical

*I Know, I Know, I Only Pray to You
When I'm in Deep Shit: The Musical*

*But Come On, Give a Sister a Break! I Mean,
I'm Wearing Out-of-Season Novelty Underwear
'Cause It's Cheaper Than Ones with the Ass Cheeks
Filled in: The Porn.*

The Ass Cheeks are Missing!: The Porn

What am I Saying?: The Musical

What is This Poem About?: The Musical

What Point Am I Trying to Prove Here?: The Musical

*Ass Cheeks are Missing AND a Movie Titled Beavie McBeaver?
Don't I Realize High School Kids Read My Work?
What is Wrong With Me?!: The Musical*

What Am I Saying to Children?: The Musical

What the Hell Am I Saying Period?!: The Musical

*I Guess What I'm Saying Is
That I Still Have a Sense of Humor: the Musical*

*I Mean, Life Can't Be That Bad If I Can Still Laugh
About It Right?: The Musical*

Maybe This Will All Turn Out Positive In the End: The Musical

God Doesn't Give you Anything You Can't Handle.
That's What "American Idol" Kelly Clarkson says,
and She Wouldn't Lie. Not Kelly Clarkson,
Not Kelly: The Porn

So I Guess I'm Poor: The Musical

But Happy: The Musical.

And Until The Money Starts Rolling In: The Porn

I Guess Life As It Stands Right Now
Is Pretty Cool: The Musical.

6.) My last idea is a high concept piece:
It's about a poet who works at a coffee shop and hosts a kick ass
reading series and writes and writes and writes and works and works
and works and loves and loves and loves and is happy in her own
small way.

Also, she can shoot fireballs out of her pussy and can make all of her
ex-boyfriends gay at will.

It's called *Kalla-Kalla-Kazaam, Motherfucker!* And it's based on a true
story.

TO WHOM IT MAY CONCERN

Hello, my name is Cristin O'Keefe Aptowicz
and I am writing to you in regard
to the job opening you posted
on the HotJobs.com website,
the Monster.com website,
the EntertainmentCareers.com website,
Tisch School of the Arts Job Bulletin,
the NYU Job Bulletin or
the New York New Media Association newsletter.

I believe that my extensive office experience,
devotion to the arts, exceptional writing ability,
tireless work ethic, organizational, multi-tasking
and communication skills, amazing familiarity
with your company, and boundless vitality

would make me a great candidate for the position
of writer, developmental assistant, personal assistant,
web producer, paid intern, bartender, barrista, burrito-
maker or receptionist at your company/companies.

However, you didn't think so...
which is probably why you didn't hire me.
But guess what? I get the last laugh here, buck-o!
Because I am going to be a full-time poet!

Ha! Ha! *Ha!*

Oh, that's right! Can't change your decision now.
Can't manipulate the time/space continuum
or jump in that alternate reality machine
you saw on *Star Trek*. Nope, I'm going to be
a full-time poet and you can just suck on it.

Envious? Are you? As you sit behind your desk
with your healthcare, and your 401Ks,
and your 'guaranteed' paychecks and your ability
to tell your parents what you do for a living
without 'apologizing'?

Well, you shouldn't have fucked with me.
Suckers, I wanted to go corporate. I did.
I spent 4 months of my life—this whole summer—
in a computer lab, in a basement, doing research
to find jobs, to perfect the language in my resume
and cover letters, and not writing poetry.

I impeccably clothed, coifed and caffeinated
myself for your interviews: sharpening my wit
into the spike that would eventually nail the decision
to hire me into your brain, making you think I'm perfect
for this job, that you couldn't live without me.

But like the Backstreet Boys,
you kept playing games with my heart.

And four months later, with my entire life savings
in the tank, I began to think that you were trying
to teach me a lesson. And corporate world,
you made me sad. Very sad.

You made me think that my life had been a mistake.
That I shouldn't have studied writing. That my working class
parents shouldn't have believed in me, let me think I could be
the first person for at least four generations not to work
for a factory or for the government. Made me think it was
a mistake to even assume I could live in this city
with only words and heart and elbow grease. No rich parents,
no doting boyfriends, no MBA as a safety net.

You made me buy pantyhose!

You made me buy high heel shoes and a blow dryer!
You made me unrecognizable to myself in the mirror,
and still think: *Not good enough.*

But guess what? I discovered something.
I discovered that this life is mine. And this brain is mine.
And this talent is mine too. And it was my dumb-ass
low self-confidence that made me laugh at your jokes
and stoop to your level and hate myself that much more
with every rejection letter I got.

That was my fault. I was the one who forgot
my self-worth. But it's your fault you never saw it.
And your loss you never hired it. And your words
that you will eat when I buy ramen noodles in bulk,
and struggle to pay rent, and use soap as shampoo,
and salt as soap, and begin mistaking my friends'
couches for luxury hotels where I can stay for free.

Because I'll be doing all of it with a big smile on my face
and a big caffeinated heart surging in my ribcage
and self-confidence as impenetrable as the office glass
that will prevent you from feeling sunlight on your skin
from 9am to 5pm every day, Monday through Friday,
until you retire or die.

Because I am going to be a full-time poet.
Put that in your IPO and smoke it!

THINGS I HAVE FORGOTTEN TO PACK

Underwear
Socks
Pants without stains on them
Shirts without curse words on them
Heart medication
Warm clothing
Cool clothing
My contact person's name and number
My passport
The poem I wanted to perform
The poem I was requested to perform
My other shoe

THE GIRLS WHO PICK ME UP AT THE AIRPORT

are all unforgivably adorable.
It's true. And I am a novice still,

so I never remember to ask
for names or photos, arriving

at strange airports hopeful
that someone remembered

the New York poet they ordered
online like a vulgar bouquet.

But the girls who pick me up
at the airport are easy to spot.

I always say, thank God
I'm a woman, because

I don't know if I could handle,
as a man, the arrogance

these coincidences build,
as I swagger up to the cutest girl

in the joint, swing my backpack
over my shoulder and say,

Hi, I'm Cristin, any chance
you are here for me?

TO THE GIRL WORKING THE CAFÉ DURING MY READING

I know you can hear me,
because you laugh when my poetry
gets dirty, which it frequently does.

And based on this laugh, I'd wager I'm not
the first poet who's come through here to have a crush
on you, and I won't be the last,

what with your short dyed red hair,
impossibly small nose ring, your soft
grey tee-shirt advertising a band

so cool I've never heard of them before.
And I bet you have a boyfriend
waiting for you somewhere, because

you are beautiful, sparkling,
and generous with your laughter
and with your coffee. I, too, have

a boyfriend, but let's forget about them
for a moment. This poem is not about
boyfriends. This poem is about you.

You, who wait until I finish a poem
to steam milk. You, who giggle like
cool sugar in hot foam. You, who

probably work too hard and too long
for too little tips and yet still smile at me
until your nose wrinkles. Thank you

for the small perfect gift of your face,
for the soft thunder of your hands,
for making this touring poet feel

right at home.

ODE TO COLLEGE CAFETERIAS

They say that your college years
are the best years of your life.

Don't believe it. This is the same line
they tried to feed you about high school.

And I hope you've learned the truth about that.
But I will give college this: you will never again

be exposed to so many awesome cafeteria options.
I don't want to scare you, current college students,

but please know that omelet stations in your future
will not be so abundant with fresh vegetables.

One day soon, you will find yourself staring
at a potato bar with only two or three fixings,

and prepare yourself for the fact that none of them
will be vegan. Appreciate it now, or regret it later,

I say. For one day you too, will be 25 years old
drinking coffee you paid for and made yourself,

staring into your bowl of Special K and thinking:
I can't believe I only have one milk option!

I can't believe it's 8am and I can't just pour
some fresh soft serve ice cream on this tasty bitch.

HOTEL ROOM

I will never grow tired of the hotel rooms.
I don't mind the thin sheets, the drafty windows,
the high school swimming team getting drunk
in the room next door, the wake-up calls
that don't happen, the drapes that don't close,
the toilets that run, the showers that drip, the stains
you wish you could stop trying to identify.

For working class girls, there is still
something vaguely princess-y about hotel rooms.
Beds you can jump on, coffee cups you don't
have to wash, sheets you don't need to tuck,
the all-night miracle of a TV with more
than five channels. I can't help it that I am
still charmed by this small gesture.

Grateful, the next morning I always fill out
the comments cards: I had a wonderful time,
the service was great, the rooms were clean,
I'd gladly recommend to all my friends and family
this Holiday Inn in Hastings, Nebraska.

THE PLANE RIDES THERE AND BACK

I admit, you do feel like a bit of a badass.
Your three sets of clothes: travel, bedtime
and performance. Your packed books for sale
and your laptop in case you are moved to write.

Poetry has put me on more airplanes than
weddings, family reunions, vacations,
or all of those combined. I'd never have believed it
if you told me. Even now, on the flights out,

my heart stirs, a nervous twitching, a state of disbelief.
Somewhere co-workers turn on their computers,
somewhere a boyfriend sleeps off his night shift.
And I am in the air, I am above the city, flying.

The trip home is different, obviously. I am
classically over-eager at these things: my voice
grounded down to rasp overnight, my body
absolutely and unforgivably limp, as if I worked

a real job in the last twenty-four hours. It's not easy,
I'm not saying that: the long flights, the odd hours,
the new faces, the lumpy beds, but let's be honest.
This is not work. And so sometimes, the flight home

can feel like an absolution. Eyes closed, breathing
slowed, I think: one day I'll write a poem good enough
to have earned this time in the air, these hours shining
in a brief bright sun.

THINGS I CANNOT SAY TO YOU,
MALE COLLEGE SPOKEN WORD POET
WHO I'M SUPPOSED TO BE HELPING OUT

Stop being such a pussy.
Stop whining when you don't get
what you want the first time out.

You either need to learn to spell,
or learn how to turn on
the "spell check" function
on your computer.

Stop thinking that bedazzling
your clichés will make them
not clichés. It just makes them
gaudier clichés.

I know you want to move
out of your comfort zone,
but I don't want to read
your persona poem
about Hurricane Katrina
when your only research was
other people's persona poems
about Hurricane Katrina.

This must be said:
looking & dressing like
a Bob's Big Boy figurine
doesn't automatically prove
you are a nice guy.

Relatedly, being short doesn't mean you
can stare at women's boobs
all the time.

Just so you know,
your hip hop poem was actually *racist*.
Your poem about your grandmother,
actually *ageist*! And your poem titled
"Celebratin' Women" was actually so
misogynistic it was like being hit in the face
with a bottle of vinegar douche.

Look, I know I am coming at you
pretty strong, but know that I want
to help you. I want to help you so hard.
I want to punch that help right into
your stupid, privileged face.

Know that more than anything,
I want your horrible poetry to give birth
to some really good poetry.

So please, focus on these four points:
    1.) Listen to what your workshop is telling you.
    2.) Read more books.
    3.) YouTube is not a book!
    4.) And remember that our eyes and
          our brains are located up here.

MIGRATORY PATTERNS
OF NORTH AMERICAN SONGBIRDS

I was walking across campus at a fancy prep school
where I was being paid to perform poetry to students
wearing much more expensive shoes than mine,
and I couldn't believe children of such privilege

could be so rude, letting their cell phones shrilly
ring and ring and ring, ceaseless and loud, echoing.
The students were all too absorbed in each other,
the warm air and their fresh sweat. But the ringing:

it was driving me crazy! So I stomped around, swinging
my glare like a battle axe, packing my frustration
like a cigarette I was ready to smoke. It was then
I realized: the stupid racket, it wasn't cell phones.

It was, in fact, several trees full of cocksure birds
singing, loud and lustful, for their potential mates.
It was spring, and I hadn't even noticed. *Those birds*,
I said, laughing, *I thought they were cell phones!*

I mean, I thought their songs were ring tones!
And the students looked at me, then at the birds,
and, after passing me forgiving smiles, returned
to their heat, their own songs. They kicked each

other, spun each other around, pounding keypads
with hot fingers, and waited, damp and smiling.
And the birds, they kept on singing. And me?
I walked to class, slowly. It was spring,

and it seemed like we all suddenly remembered
what we were placed on this earth to do.

FIRST WORDS

Before they grew older and, I suppose,
knew better, poets I've read seemed to really
like the word *archipelago*. I find it repeated

in a lot of well-known poets' early books.
That's what I do for fun. Read first works
by poets and try to find the common words.

I'm that type of girl. *Verdant* is another
commonly repeated word, as is *moon*.
What is it that makes poets fall so quickly

out of love with the moon, banishing it
from later books, focusing instead
on the enduring sun, its failsafe ability to rise

and set according to the metaphor, its desire
to burn the broad shoulders of distant
fathers. As for me? I discovered the word

discordant (and its misspelled sister,
dischordant) have tracked their snowy boots
into my early verse. My trembling emotions

were *discordant*. My hopeless love life,
tearfully *discordant*. My jittery legs,
mumbling conversations? *Discordant*, all,

and don't you forget it. If only I'd read more,
if only I knew that all the answers my poetry
ever needed for my nascent, discordant life

could be found in the lush, verdant moon,
plopped humming in the night sky. If only
I'd looked up, joined that twinkling archipelago

of dead poets, platters in hand, licking their lips,
murmuring, *My God, it's so good! How is it
that we could have forgotten for so long?*

FACTORY

For Jim Daniels

The boys on the line come up:
This your last day? You quitting?
He nods. They wink.
from "Odie's Last Day"

You were my first real poet, the first I claimed
as my own, the first I saw write about my world:
the factories, the men inside, the spit and machines,
about your father's shirt, armpits stiff and yellow,

how you ached to be nestled into them.
I loved the grit of you, how you studied poetry
and returned each summer to the factory,
how I couldn't tell if you did it because

you had to or wanted to. I knew the taste
of that drug: knowing the value of your muscle,
your heart's tug when classmates wrote
about their summers stuck in houses,

how they fell in love and it ruined them,
how good it felt to know your blood
is tougher than theirs. So you can imagine
my anger's salty rush when I read the poems

where you grew up, when you left the factory
and became a professor, when you married,
when you raised children who would never know
this rusty metal life. I seethed at your new work,

your poems about Italy— *Italy!* —and clean hair
and good wine, poems which made me face
the piping hot mirror of ambition, the shiny heat
that seemed to be generated by reward,

by the simple conclusion that someone could
live a life they deserved. Jim, I'm sorry your poetry
became my conspiracy, my bible, my assurance
that it was alright to never leave. I'm sorry

at how I can still bristle at the image of you,
clean and dry, standing before a classroom
full of the type of students we hated.
But most of all, I'm sorry that some nights,

I refuse your beautiful new work entirely, returning
you to your factory, shoving your hands into gloves,
pushing you to a machine, whispering, *Now then,
doesn't this feel better? Now doesn't this feel right?*

SEXTON AND PLATH

After handing me *The Bell Jar*,
my mother half-joked, "Now don't
go sticking your head in an oven
after reading this, okay?"

It seemed like easy enough advice.
Young, life was something I fought for.
I couldn't conceive of your shared desire,
to want to give up your breath like a bribe.

I wish I could have told you that we
would have remembered you anyway.
But instead, furious, I add your names
to the maddening list my heart catalogues,

women who ripped life from their mouths
on purpose, a generation of artists who
lynched themselves: Karen Carpenter's
teeth of nails, Janis Joplin's purple fists,

Frida Kahlo's stomach of blood,
Diane Arbus' flashing silver eyes,
and of course, you, Anne and Sylvia,
your names having become the definition

of what it means to be woman and poet,
the long beautiful death of it, 'the awful
rowing towards God.' I hate the silence
of your final books, posthumously published,

half suicide notes, half testaments of what
could have been. I read your collected works
like slow-motion train wrecks, like videos
where I can rewind to the good parts,

when your children seemed enough
to keep you together. When your words
galloped out of you rough, a sky absolute
and seeping with sun. Working my way

backwards through the pages, I fall in love
with all that is difficult and bone, poetry
as hot breath and glass, a terrible coming
and coming apart. I want to thank you

for that honesty, and in the same pulse,
rip into you for that weakness. I want nothing
but for you to live. I'm sorry I am not
strong enough to see past the end,

that all your beautiful, hard lines close
for me on the same images: you, both,
passive and purposeful, breathing in
your poisoned air. I cannot forgive you

for giving up. Your words are not enough
to suspend this heartbreak, this shaking
in my spine and breasts. That you took
all that was wild and beautiful and woman,

and silenced it. That you thought of death
as something you did, when really, it was
proof of nothing, a showcase of your abilities
to sit submissive and wait, death leaking in.

Meanwhile, a chorus of blood and paper
daughters orphaned, a dumb lesson taught:
that nothing is more important than
everything, your last bitter breath exhaled.

DARGER

What we know of you is finite,
pieced from your diaries and journals
and a document called *MY LIFE HISTORY*,
that you wrote for years without crossing out
nearly a single word. Any good historian
could dash out the details: your Chicago birth,
your crippled father, the childhood spent
in institutions, orphaned, adulthood spent
working silent in hospitals, your lonely life
to death, sure, sure, sure. But what no one
can figure out is your mad purpose,
what made you return and return and return
to your art. Is that even what you called it?
Who knows? Your landlord, a failed artist
himself, inherited your work by default,
rooms of your mania wrought true.

They call your life's work *Outsider Art*,
because you created without influence,
without critique, and it all could have
ended up in the garbage, I suppose,
and no one would have known better.
Art Brut, Raw Art, Rough Art,
they've even called it *Art of the Insane*,
and what does this say about me, who locks
admiration in the bird cage of my mouth?

I confess I've envied your violent world:
its blood and wings, its avenging little girls;
envied the years you spent manifesting it,
the seamless nights you spent getting it
absolutely right, despite that inevitable quiet

at each end. Not one person who loves you now
ever said it to your breathing face.

You are a miracle and the mystery to me is not
whether you knew that people would eventually
come to appreciate what you did. The secret
I want to release is how you didn't seem to care
if they ever did.

SCHADENFREUDE

If we are being honest here,
then I can tell you I never wanted
your books to do well.

At readings, I thrill at the silence
which greets your attempts at wit,
the restless sighs and stretches

your poetry invites, the teacup
of applause an audience politely
serves you. When your name

goes unrecognized, when your work
is ignored, my delirious heart
rings its most shameful bell.

If we are being honest here, know
that I never liked your face, never
liked your handwriting, never

thought your stories were that
interesting. If we are being honest here,
let me confess that the mere knowledge

of your existence has literally ruined
entire cups of coffee for me. If we are
being honest here, then know this:

the thing for which I am most grateful
is that you have never seen me in my low
points: the indifferent audiences,

the flamboyant typos, my cowering ego.
The debt I most owe some forgiving god
for this simple miracle:

that you have never seen the way
my whole body flinches every time I hear
a line I wish I'd been good enough to write.

POEM WRITTEN ON COLD MEDICATION

Sounds like a fun idea. The bell of my face
filled with the sleeping doves of illness, my tongue
fuzzy with down. The cold medicine didn't really
clear anything out, as much as it sharpened the fog,
static still static, only clearer on a different channel.
Last night, we ate Thai food to help clear my head.
It didn't work, and this morning, I shat fire.

MOON PARTY

There is a house in the middle of our street
which has a large silver banner in its window.
The banner reads MOON PARTY. The banner
never comes down. We stare into the windows
and see real silverware, clean sneakers lined up
against the wall, an impressively large teeter-totter
topped with a smiling hamburger face displayed
on a bookshelf. This house throws a party about
once a month. The people who attend these parties
are always better dressed than us.

DIVISION OF LABOR

It has been decided that I will be the one
who wakes up before 8am to go to the office job,
and you will be the one who wakes up around 2pm
to sling beers at your bar. This works well for us,
as I love the taste of coffee and you can tolerate drunks.
We both will be the ones to hustle our poetry, splitting
our throats raw, lugging our unsold books home, hopeful.

At the end of the week, we pile our money together.
We treat it like sleeping pigeons, knowing how quickly
it can take off when scared. We are doing all right,
better than all right, probably, yet sometimes I stare hard
at my plate, at the new comforter on a friend's bed,
at their happy tans, their lucky dogs, their cats
who eat organic food. Sometimes I want to tattoo
I'm going to be poor forever over my slumped shoulders,
as I flop home in my broken-soled shoes, tugging at threads.

My lover laughs though, and so do I, I guess. Yes, yes.
Sometimes we still cook popcorn for dinner. We like
to walk there if we can. We aren't ones to leave a penny
lying in the street like a hit and run, like a damaged stray.
But we are good tippers, we are good lovers,
we are good laughers, and we still write.

TO INSURE PROMPT SERVICE

Before my boyfriend moved in with me, my old roommate
had two nicknames for the Neptune Diner's longtime waiters:
Surly Thick and Surly Bald. She was one of those people
who believed that tips had to be earned through good service.

My boyfriend, who moved in when my old roommate left
for Australia—a place, coincidentally, which does not believe
in tipping—quickly explained that the ratio is reversed:
good tipping ensures good service. And great tipping, well,

means that we were called by our first names as soon as we
entered the joint, that our cups of soup were instantly upgraded
to bowls, that we could have hot rolls whenever we asked
instead of the sad baskets of potato bread. Great tipping means

never having to ask for refills for our water, never being sat
next to a high-octane toddler, never the wrongly cooked meat
or the wrongly filled omelet. Great tipping also means that
when one of my oldest friends in the world came to visit

and he and I came to the diner just the two of us, to split
a slice of cheesecake and a couple of strong dark coffees,
that come breakfast time the next morning, both waiters
came over to my boyfriend before we had even placed our order

and told him: *Last night, she came in with another man.*
My boyfriend thanked them by name, *Gregory, Frankie,*
theatrically cracking his knuckles. That Christmas, they
received cards from both of us, two 20's tucked neatly inside.

BILLY COLLINS

Inspired, perhaps, by my frustrated sighs,
my boyfriend turned and offered me this:
Well, you know, Billy Collins once said
that if you are stuck in a poem, you should
just have a dog walk into the poem, because
people love dogs. Why don't you try that?

Yeah, why don't I try that? I snapped,
Because I'm sure that will solve everything:
just have a dog walk into the poem. Perfect.
I'll get on that right away.

Well, maybe it would help, he replied.
You never know. Maybe I've never told you,
but maybe your poetry needs more dogs.
Maybe it's been seriously lacking regarding
dogs for a long, long time.

Oh really? I said, looking up from my laptop.
Well maybe you should break up with me
and start dating Billy Collins! Because then
everybody's problems would be solved.
And you'd get all the dog poetry you need!

Well, maybe I will, he barked, maybe
I will start dating Billy Collins. Because
Billy Collins seems like a really nice guy.
I like his poetry. He looks good in sweaters.

He glared at me. I glared right back.
Time passed. And suddenly, out of nowhere,
a dog walked into the room.

BARFLY

Last night, you came home so drunk,
you appeared hammered even in my dreams.
In the dream, important people from my past
gaped at the doorway of our bedroom, jamming
their fingers in their ears, yelling, *God, he is
so drunk!* Last night, you snored so garishly,
that the shaggy cats we were cat-sitting
began spontaneously fighting. It was anarchy,
an all-cat version of Altamont, and your chokes
and gurgles and snorts were the Rolling Stones,
man. This morning, I woke up five minutes
before the alarm was set to go off and I thought,
Aw, fuck it. Went to my computer and found
you had left me a hot, limp pickle wrapped
in saran wrap laying next to my keyboard.

DRUNK BOYFRIEND
ON A FRIDAY MORNING

This morning, as I was getting ready for work,
my bartender boyfriend, still tipsy from last

night's shift, suddenly woke up and asked me,
Where am I? What's going on? And I told him,

You're fine, it's just me. I'm just getting ready
to leave for work. And he was like,

You have to work? Why? And I was like,
I know, right? And then he closed his eyes

and solemnly asked, Is it Sunday or Monday?
And I was like, What? And he was like,

Is it Sunday? Is it Monday? Are you sure
you have to go to work? And I'm like,

It's *Friday*. And yes, I have to go to work.
And you are going to have to go to work

tonight too. And he was like, Wait, now
I understand. And I was like, Understand what?

And he was like, For a minute there,
I thought I was in Heaven. And I was like,

What? Really? And he was like, Yeah,
it felt like Heaven for a minute there.

And I was like, Wait, in your vision
of Heaven, I still have to go to work?

And he was like, Yeah, but not on Sundays.
That's why I was double-checking.

THE BARTENDER'S WIFE

Night has always been this thing
on the other side of the window,
this bad novel, this dark brute
shaking the stars into clarity.

I liked dusk all right, the sun
getting down on one knee
like a gentleman to kiss my cheeks
goodbye, but the rest of it

I could always live without,
preferring coffee-scented morning
in all its dowdy soberness,
the simple hopeful stretch of it.

Last winter, a woman's heart spat
blood all over the sidewalk, a gun's
wet answer to her pointed question:
What are you going to do, kill me?

and my boyfriend was cleaning up
spilled beer and torn napkins
five city blocks away, his cell phone
thudding dully in his coat pocket.

I'm not an idiot. It's New York City
and what doesn't seem dangerous?
The book bag doubles as a bomb,
the moody teen as trigger finger.

Hell, even the skyline can look as sharp
and anonymous as knives, your dumb
consistent breath proof only that luck
had negotiated your way out of being

at the wrong place at the wrong time
again. But it's New York City and there
are times and places when even luck
would throw its silver fingers in the air.

Still, each morning, I find him sleeping
next to me like the beautiful answer
to a stupid question: he's there.
He's there like he's always there,

and I don't know who to thank for it all,
whose generous hands are placed
protective on his shoulders, guiding him
back to me again and again.

Who lets the bright light of my worry,
my heart's terrible export, shine on
as a beacon, a smoldering lighthouse
in this city's unforgiving ocean of night.

QAPARHA!

A Lovesong for J.P. Seasholtz

When you and I announced that we would be moving in together, everyone came to me with shiny platters of advice, the usual fare: that moving in together changes everything, that there's no turning back, that I'd have to accept the real you.

And I said, of course, I know, I understand.

But when I said that I would accept you, all of you, I did not realize that would include your vintage pez dispenser collection. Or your numerous bootleg tapes of Star Wars fan animation. Or that one morning I would wake to find that you had attached mini Millennium Falcons to pieces of wire, and attached said wire to suction cups, and attached said suction cups to our bathroom mirror so that I could wake up and feel as if I were brushing my teeth in an inter-galactic space battle.

These things I did not take into consideration, I admit it.

See, loving a nerd like you is like loving America, that is, if America also collected *The Incredible Mr. Limpet* comic book series and if America could often be found tipsy at 5am watching the episode where the Jetsons meet the Flintstones on DVD, which you purchased yourself and was not given as a gift. And is that a tear in your eye that I'm spying, America, when you realize the parable about that episode, that friendship and family transcend even time? Or at least that's what you'd write in your live journal, drunk.

I am living with a Nerd. And ain't nobody got advice for that.

But see, where I grew up, Nerd meant something different. I know the clank on chest of seven hard earned academic decathlon medals, including a perfect score for "interview," the only time ever in state competition, bitches. I, too, would scoff at the frequent and completely unnecessary use of the Tesla coil in movies involving

Scientists. I mean, really, who do they think they're kidding? And in my circle, we welcomed the day we got off after prom since it meant more time to study for our French AP test.

These were the Nerds that I was familiar with: the ones with anemia and scoliosis, who petitioned to let java be accepted as their foreign language credit, the ones for whom SATs were fun.

But Shap, you are a different breed altogether.

You are a Geek, and now our house is a war between the two tribes, two pale and socially inept tribes who never get laid. My tribe is losing this war.

My complete works of Richard Feynman are being displaced with vintage H.R. PufnStuf vinyl dolls, there are *Planet of the Apes* Band-Aids in my first aid kit, and when one opens up our freezer, they will find a posse of "Homies" collectible action figures, and if one should question what they are doing in there, Shappy will answer "Chillin'."

But honestly, it would be a lie to say it isn't all worth it.

Had you ever asked me before to describe whom I thought would come and live in this beaten down ribcage of mine, I would never have chosen a 35-year-old who still eats SweeTarts,

who quotes *The Simpsons* in Valentine's Day cards and condescendingly sneers at passing teenagers in cars who yell, "You're pretty out of shape to be Superman!" while you snort back, "Idiots, they don't even realize this is a Bizarro Superman t-shirt."

But you are here anyway.

And not only do you live in this heart, but you own the damn place, proof that Nerds and Geeks can find common ground somewhere other than our high school nurse's office and alone in our basements on prom night.

And if you can accept me for who I am, always littering our house with endless drafts of grant applications, barking at you if you turn off *Nightline*, and never ever washing the dishes, then I guess I can accept you in all of your Ebay-loving, thrift-store ransacking, eating-Quisp-Cereal-at-midnight glory.

This poem, as silly as it is, was written to show that which you shall forever know: *QaparHa'!*

Which is Klingon for "I love you," something I never thought I would translate, nor say out loud, but I guess that's what you do to me: Inspire me.

So *QaParha*, Jeff, and *Heghlu'meH QaQ jajvam* which means, "Thank you."

Actually it means, "Today is a good day to die."

But you'll just have to forgive me. Unlike us, the Klingons never seem to know when they have it good.

DISCONNECTED

I wonder if the reason there is not more poetry written
about the internet is because we, poets, would prefer
to be timeless, not of any age, let alone this shameless era
where the faces of your ex-boyfriends can manifest
with a click on your laptop, where Google's tempting
crystal ball promises vilification, only to show you
the untrammeled success of all your childhood nemeses,

which I admit, I thought would be childhood 'nemesi'
until my computer dictionary highlighted my stupidity.
Not the first time, I'm sure not the last; the scarlet WWW
I should wear on my chest, marking me as mad, unable
to deny my own wanderlust, searching my name online,
pawing through my stats, looking for another cupcake
to stuff into my ego's greedy mouth.

What did artists do before the internet?

Created their art, I suppose. Or cleaned their bathtubs,
cooked their meals, went to war, wrote and mailed
actual letters, rattled in their beds with consumption,
drank until dizzy, made love until dawn, or maybe
they did even simpler things: just stole outside
and sucked in that fresh blue-black night air to marvel
at the persistence of our bright, dumb moon, to stumble
tipsy into the path of an old lover, to stop and smile,
and to apologize, before stepping out of the way
and moving on.

ACKNOWLEDGMENTS

Grateful acknowledgements are made to the following journals in which some of these writings first appeared in slightly different forms:

Concise Delight – "Sex Appeal"

Criminal Class Review – "Schadenfreude"

Danse Macabre – "Darger"

Dinosaur Bees – "The Happy Fun of Love"

Frigg – "Green Umbrella" and "Thank you For Your Interest In Our Fellowship"

La Petite Zine – "Moon Party," "Close Out Sale" and "Poem Written on Cold Medication"

Poetry Quarterly – "Billy Collins"

The Foundling Review – "Division of Labor"

The Serotonin Factory – "Ode to My Morning Cup of Coffee"

Used Furniture Review – "In the Movie of My Life I Sometimes Imagine" and "Bar Fly"

Yes, Poetry – "Dear Whoever Is Sending Pictures to My Phone" and "The Bartender's Wife"

Additionally, grateful acknowledgements are made to the following print and CD anthologies, in which some of the following poems have also appeared:

Bowery Women (YBK Publishers) – "To Whom It May Concern"

An Evening of Taylor Mali & Friends (DVD) – "To The Person Who Said Funny Poetry Ain't Poetry"

Indiefeed Performance Poetry Podcast (performancepoetry.indiefeed. com) – "Ode to My Morning Cup of Coffee," "All I'd Leave Behind" and "Sexton and Plath"

Urbana: Best of 2004 (CD) – "To The Person Who Said Funny Poetry Ain't Poetry "

Lastly, grateful acknowledgements are made to **Steve Marsh** and **The Wordsmith Press**, who published an earlier edition of this book.

ABOUT THE AUTHOR

CRISTIN O'KEEFE APTOWICZ is the author of four other books of poetry: *Dear Future Boyfriend, Hot Teen Slut, Oh, Terrible Youth* and *Everything is Everything*. She is also the author of the non-fiction book, *Words In Your Face: A Guided Tour Through Twenty Years of the New York City Poetry Slam*, which *The Washington Post* named as one of five Notable Books on Exploring Poetry in 2008. Born and raised in Philadelphia, Aptowicz moved to New York City at the age of 17. At age 19, she founded the three-time National Poetry Slam championship poetry series NYC-Urbana, which is still held weekly at the NYC's famed Bowery Poetry Club. Most recently, Aptowicz was named the 2010-2011 ArtsEdge Writer-In-Residence at the University of Pennsylvania and was also awarded a 2011 National Endowment for the Arts Fellowship in Poetry.

For more information, please visit her website:
www.aptowicz.com

NEW WRITE BLOODY BOOKS FOR 2011

DEAR FUTURE BOYFRIEND
A Write Bloody reissue of Cristin O'Keefe Aptowicz's first book of poetry

HOT TEEN SLUT
A Write Bloody reissue of Cristin O'Keefe Aptowicz's second book of poetry
about her time writing for porn

WORKING CLASS REPRESENT
A Write Bloody reissue of Cristin O'Keefe Aptowicz's third book of poetry

OH, TERRIBLE YOUTH
A Write Bloody reissue of Cristin O'Keefe Aptowicz's fourth book of poetry
about her terrible youth

38 BAR BLUES
A collection of poems by C.R .Avery

WORKIN' MIME TO FIVE
Humor by Derrick Brown

REASONS TO LEAVE THE SLAUGHTER
New poems by Ben Clark

YESTERDAY WON'T GOODBYE
New poems by Brian Ellis

WRITE ABOUT AN EMPTY BIRDCAGE
New poems by Elaina M. Ellis

THESE ARE THE BREAKS
New prose by Idris Goodwin

BRING DOWN THE CHANDELIERS
New poems by Tara Hardy

THE FEATHER ROOM
New poems by Anis Mojgani

LOVE IN A TIME OF ROBOT APOCALYPSE
New poems by David Perez

THE NEW CLEAN
New poems by Jon Sands

THE UNDISPUTED GREATEST WRITER OF ALL TIME
New poems by Beau Sia

SUNSET AT THE TEMPLE OF OLIVES
New poems by Paul Suntup

GENTLEMAN PRACTICE
New poems by Buddy Wakefield

HOW TO SEDUCE A WHITE BOY IN TEN EASY STEPS
New poems by Laura Yes Yes

OTHER WRITE BLOODY BOOKS (2003 - 2010)

STEVE ABEE, GREAT BALLS OF FLOWERS (2009)
New poems by Steve Abee

EVERYTHING IS EVERYTHING (2010)
New poems by Cristin O'Keefe Aptowicz

CATACOMB CONFETTI (2010)
New poems by Josh Boyd

BORN IN THE YEAR OF THE BUTTERFLY KNIFE (2004)
Poetry collection, 1994-2004 by Derrick Brown

I LOVE YOU IS BACK (2006)
Poetry compilation (2004-2006) by Derrick Brown

SCANDALABRA (2009)
New poetry compilation by Derrick Brown

DON'T SMELL THE FLOSS (2009)
New Short Fiction Pieces By Matty Byloos

THE BONES BELOW (2010)
New poems by Sierra DeMulder

THE CONSTANT VELOCITY OF TRAINS (2008)
New poems by Lea C. Deschenes

HEAVY LEAD BIRDSONG (2008)
New poems by Ryler Dustin

UNCONTROLLED EXPERIMENTS IN FREEDOM (2008)
New poems by Brian Ellis

CEREMONY FOR THE CHOKING GHOST (2010)
New poems by Karen Finneyfrock

POLE DANCING TO GOSPEL HYMNS (2008)
Poems by Andrea Gibson

CITY OF INSOMNIA (2008)
New poems by Victor D. Infante

THE LAST TIME AS WE ARE (2009)
New poems by Taylor Mali

IN SEARCH OF MIDNIGHT: THE MIKE MCGEE HANDBOOK OF AWESOME (2009)
New poems by Mike McGee

OVER THE ANVIL WE STRETCH (2008)
New poems by Anis Mojgani

ANIMAL BALLISTICS (2009)
New poems by Sarah Morgan

NO MORE POEMS ABOUT THE MOON (2008)
NON-Moon poems by Michael Roberts

MILES OF HALLELUJAH (2010)
New poems by Rob "Ratpack Slim" Sturma

SPIKING THE SUCKER PUNCH (2009)
New poems by Robbie Q. Telfer

RACING HUMMINGBIRDS (2010)
New poems by Jeanann Verlee

LIVE FOR A LIVING (2007)
New poems by Buddy Wakefield

WRITE BLOODY ANTHOLOGIES

THE ELEPHANT ENGINE HIGH DIVE REVIVAL (2009)
Poetry by Buddy Wakefield, Derrick Brown,
Anis Mojgani, Shira Erlichman and many more!

THE GOOD THINGS ABOUT AMERICA (2009)
An illustrated, un-cynical look at our American Landscape. Various authors.
Edited by Kevin Staniec and Derrick Brown

JUNKYARD GHOST REVIVAL (2008)
Poetry by Andrea Gibson, Buddy Wakefield, Anis Mojgani,
Derrick Brown, Robbie Q, Sonya Renee and Cristin O'Keefe Aptowicz

THE LAST AMERICAN VALENTINE:
ILLUSTRATED POEMS TO SEDUCE AND DESTROY (2008)
24 authors, 12 illustrators team up for a collection of non-sappy love poetry.
Edited by Derrick Brown

LEARN THEN BURN (2010)
Anthology of poems for the classroom. Edited by Tim Stafford and Derrick Brown.

LEARN THEN BURN TEACHER'S MANUAL (2010)
Companion volume to the *Learn Then Burn* anthology. Includes lesson plans and worksheets for educators.
Edited by Tim Stafford and Molly Meacham.

WWW.WRITEBLOODY.COM

WRITEBLOODY
QUALITY AMERICAN BOOKS

PULL YOUR BOOKS UP BY THEIR BOOTSTRAPS

Write Bloody Publishing distributes and promotes great books of fiction, poetry and art every year. We are an independent press dedicated to quality literature and book design, with an office in Long Beach, CA.

Our employees are authors and artists so we call ourselves a family. Our design team comes from all over America: modern painters, photographers and rock album designers create book covers we're proud to be judged by.

We publish and promote 8-12 tour-savvy authors per year. We are grass-roots, D.I.Y., bootstrap believers. Pull up a good book and join the family. Support independent authors, artists and presses.

Visit us online:
WRITEBLOODY.COM

CPSIA information can be obtained at www.ICGtesting.com
Printed in the USA
LVOW110838031111

253350LV00001B/10/P